THE HISTORY OF TEA

To Dominique and my three children, Romain, Clément, and Julien.

Translated from the French by David Radzinowicz
Copyediting: Anne Korkeakivi
Design: Delphine Delastre
Typesetting: Barbara Kekus
Proofreading: Fui Lee Luk

Distributed in North America by Rizzoli International Publications, Inc.

Originally published in French as *L'Histoire du thé*
© Flammarion, Paris, 2006

English-language edition
© Flammarion, 2007

www.editions.flammarion.com

07 08 09 4 3 2 1
ISBN-13: 978-2-0803-0022-5
Dépôt légal: 03/2007

All photographs by Sophie Boussahba, except pp. 58–59 © Roger-Viollet

Printed in Malaysia by Tien Wah Press

CHRISTINE DATTNER

Photographs by Sophie Boussahba

Styling by Emmanuelle Javelle

THE HISTORY OF TEA

Flammarion

THE HISTORY OF TEA

INTRODUCTION

Tea, the drink of the gods and of men. Yet this beverage had a long path to follow before becoming a global phenomenon.

Camellia sinensis, better known by the name of the "tea plant," was one of the first plants cultivated on earth and has probably been around for some five thousand years. There are many myths about its discovery, although the birthplace of tea was without question China. One popular legend, that of the Emperor Chen Nung, dates to the year 2737 B.C.E.. Mightily concerned for his health, this Chinese emperor would invariably have his water boiled before drinking it. One day, after a long walk, he fell asleep under a tree. Before drifting off, however, he ordered his water to be prepared in a cauldron as usual. A light breeze rose, and a few leaves of the tree floated down into the water. When he awoke, the emperor drank a cup of this infusion and found it delicious. Thus was tea born.

For centuries, China jealously guarded the secrets of tea-growing and -making. These secrets were to spark many conflicts during history, but tea has also been responsible for bringing two worlds closer together: the East and the West.

THE ORIGINS OF TEA

CHINA

One may forgive a murder—
but a blunder in tea-making, never.
(Chinese proverb)

The precise historical origins of tea—such as the legend surrounding Emperor Chen Nung in 2737 B.C.E.—may be disputed, but China was definitely its cradle. And, it remains today the country offering the greatest diversity of this product: more than ten thousand different teas recorded. As a Chinese saying proclaims, it would take more than a lifetime to discover them all.

Over the ages, tea has been served in various ways, and as Chinese dynasty followed dynasty, each brought a new fashion in its preparation.

THE TANG DYNASTY (618–907)

During this ancient dynasty, tea was regarded as a "spiritual" drink. In this period, tea was normally "pressed" and prepared as "bricks" or "cakes" for better conservation and transport. It was also employed as a currency of exchange: the cake of tea was divided into "sections," and one simply had to snap off a piece and swap it for something else. Tea is still today manufactured in this form in certain Chinese provinces.

It was during the eighth century that the first treatise on tea was written by Lu Yu. This unfinished work explains how tea was grown, made, and consumed. At that time, part of the tea-wafer or cake was broken off, softened with a little, very hot water, and steeped. Tea nurtured body and soul, and was considered a food, an aromatic, and was a common ingredient in soups.

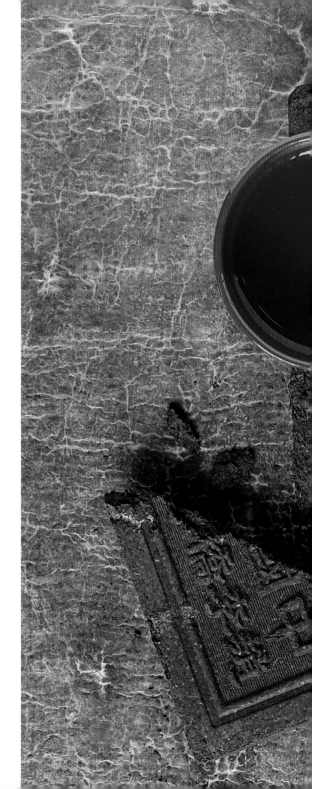

THE SUNG DYNASTY (960–1279)

It was in this era that tea was first powdered. The leaves were crushed between two grinding stones, then hot water was poured over a little of the powder produced and "beaten" with a whip until the mixture frothed. The *cha no yu* (way of tea) tea ceremony in Japan still proceeds in this manner today.

THE MING DYNASTY (1368–1644)

During this epoch, tea leaves were kept whole, and simply dried and the beverage infused. It was in this form that Westerners, by the intermediary of maritime trading companies, discovered tea in the seventeenth century.

THE QING DYNASTY (1644–1911)

By this dynasty, tea preparation and brewing techniques had been carefully mastered; the choice of water, its temperature, and the length of infusion were regulated, and particular "utensils" for tea preparation were already widely employed. Porcelain or stoneware for cups were already being manufactured in the province of Guangdong, and the first clay teapots, of the finest quality, were being produced in the province of Yixing.

During this era, tea became quite a fad. Trading companies—Dutch at the beginning, followed by the English and the French—started importing and retailing the precious leaves all over Europe. The first "caravans" brought tea from Beijing all the way to the court of the tsar at Moscow. It was at this time, thanks to the drink's popularity, that the earliest smoked teas were created "by accident."

Facing page:
A brick of tea, China.

A farmer with a big order to fill decided to accelerate the drying process by putting his tea leaves above a fire made of spruce wood. As the leaves were impregnated by the smoke, Lapsang Souchong, so popular in the West today, was born.

In 1798, the then-head of the British government, William Pitt, sent a mission to Peking to obtain commercial arrangements with China. The Chinese emperor, feeling fearful of the agreement, decided instead to close the doors of his empire to every Western tradesman. All commerce was forbidden. The English were, as a result, obliged to pay through the nose for what had become their favorite drink, and their balance of trade quickly suffered.

Since settling in their Indian colonies, the English had developed the cultivation of the poppy flower, and had adopted the practice of exchanging opium for tea and spices with the Chinese. In response to Emperor Daoguang's hostile reaction, and in the teeth of the blockade, the English opted drastically to increase illegal sales of opium to China. In Canton, whole cargoes were seized and destroyed by the Chinese government, spurring the government of Queen Victoria to indulge in a bout of gunboat diplomacy. First, Canton was attacked. Then the English went up the Yangzi Jiang to Nankin. Forced to capitulate, the emperor conceded to England free trade in the principal Chinese ports, such as Shanghai and Canton. On August 29, 1842, the treaty of Nankin, which ended the First Opium War, was signed.

Facing page: An infusion of Golden Daisy tea.

From this time on, until the revolution of October 1949, China underwent many civil wars and widespread conflicts. It was obviously the "red-haired devil" (in other words, the English), come from the West to trade in tea, who had been the cause of it all.

Mao Tse-tung's seizure of power in 1949 brought the closure of teahouses in China, as Mao held that drinking tea in such establishments was an "unproductive" activity that needed to be stamped out. Not before the mid-1990s did tearooms and tea shops reemerge in China. Today, teahouses there serve produce of excellent quality and are justly famous for their convivial atmosphere. The Chinese have rediscovered the *xian cha*: teatime, a time for doing nothing.

CHINA TODAY

The Chinese primarily consume green and semi-green teas, keeping the entire production of black tea for export. Green tea is drunk throughout the day. They often use glass jars in which tea leaves covered with hot water are placed each morning before going to work. It is this infusion, with extra water added to the same leaves, that is drunk over the course of the day. By evening, tea produced in this manner becomes very light with hardly any theine.

When they have the leisure, the Chinese enjoy two other methods of taking tea. For drinking green tea, they opt for the famous *zhong*, a china vessel with a lid and saucer. The lid symbolizes the sky, the cup the human being, and the saucer the earth. A few leaves of green tea are deposited at the bottom of the zhong. Then water, which is not too hot

(158°F/70°C), is poured over them and allowed to infuse for two to three minutes before drinking. Another method is the *gong fu cha*, or "teatime." On this occasion, a semi-fermented blue-green tea or Oolong is employed. It is prepared in a small Yixing earthenware teapot to a high concentration. The tiny bowls from which it is drunk are also made of clay, the inside being generally enameled white. Each gesture is of the utmost precision. The small teapot and tiny bowls are placed on a tray with a tank called a "boat." The whole "tea service" is then warmed, and hot water is poured into the teapot. The mixture then stands for only two to three minutes. The tea is drunk in little gulps, and several infusions are possible. The entire ceremony evokes serenity and sharing.

In China, tea represents a way of life, a philosophy and an aesthetic quest. A number of Chinese poems and legends show the importance of tea in the life of this vast country.

MAD FOR TEA

The first bowl moistens the lips and slips down the
  throat,
The second banishes all my loneliness,
The third lightens the burden of my spirit,
Sharpening the inspiration I've gathered from all the
  books I've read.
The fourth makes me perspire just a little,
Dispersing through my pores the afflictions of an
  entire life.
The fifth bowl purifies every atom in my being.
The sixth turns me into one of the immortals.
The seventh is the last… I can drink no more.
A light breeze wafts up from my armpits.
                              –Lu Tung (Tang Dynasty)

POEM TO THE TEA IN MY PAINTINGS

I buy a green mountain,
Where I grow nothing but tea plants of the first
  order.
In spring it's picking time
On every slope.
It is steeped according to tradition.
I love the aroma and flavor
My tea brings.
                              –Yan Tang (Ming Dynasty)

Facing page:
Bamboo tea box.

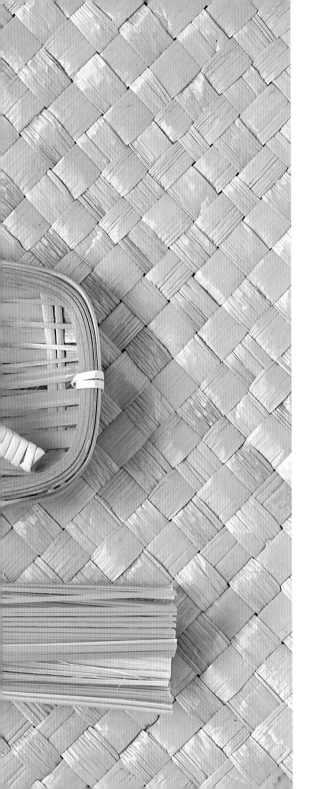

POEM

Close by the bridge made of three planks,
Some sheaves of dry mulberry branches and of
  hemp.
The Qiqiang tea-plants unfurl their twigs,
People are busy gathering in the new buds.
On the edge of the brook the girls
  work the plucked green tea.
Through the curtain over the window I can only see
  their lovely silhouette.
Their jet black hair floats over their temples,
Forgetting their home nestling at the foot of Mount
  Biluo.
As I recite the poem, I can smell a fragrance
  that makes me feel parched.
I burn with desire to drink of the new tea
  the girls prepare.

                    —Cai Tingbi (Qing Dynasty)

The Qing dynasty witnessed the birth of a delightful legend that tells of the discovery of Tie Guan Yin, the famous Oolong tea produced in the picturesque province of Fujian and, more particularly, in the district of Anxi. Every day, a farmer would walk past a small ruined temple once dedicated to the goddess Guan Yin. Its dilapidated appearance made him sigh sadly, but he did not have the means to repair the building. However, to honor the goddess, he regularly swept it, lighting a few incense sticks and cleaning the statue. One night, she appeared to him and announced that a treasure was hidden in a cave behind the temple.

Facing page:
Bamboo tea utensils.

*Lapsong Souchong,
China.*

*Facing page:
Stoneware cup and
earthenware teapot
from China.*

He was to take great care of it and share it generously with all his neighbors. The delighted peasant hurried off to the place she indicated, and was crestfallen. The only "treasure" he found were a few scattered seeds. How could he hope to share so little? Out of love for the goddess, nonetheless, he carefully planted his booty in his garden and was amazed to see a number of splendid shrubs emerge. Making an infusion of a few leaves, he discovered a miraculous drink, pure and invigorating. Brimming over with enthusiasm, he put his heart and soul into growing this tea plant so his neighbors could enjoy it too. Production increased, and the variety was dubbed "Tie Guan Yin" (the iron goddess of mercy), after the metallic statue of the goddess in the old temple. Thus, the poor farmer became a wealthy tea producer and was able to restore the temple. Still today, Tie Guan Yin remains a much sought-after Oolong.

The color of the infusion
varies a great deal from
tea to tea.

Yin Zhen (Silver Needles), a very fine white tea from the Fujian region.

Zin Zhen is a white tea. Only the top bud is plucked. Covered with a white down, it takes on a gray tinge once dried.

JAPAN

Tea was introduced to Japan in the ninth century by Buddhist monks returning from China. It was probably the monk Ei Chu who first gave a cup of tea to Emperor Saga. At that time in Japan, tea (in the form of a powder mixed with hot water and beaten with a bamboo whip) was consumed mainly by monks who drank it to keep awake during their long hours of meditation.

Not before the twelfth or thirteenth century did tea spread throughout Japan. New accessories, bowls, and cups were first imported from China: only then could the *cha no yu* (way of tea) come into being. It became a ritual that still persists in Japan. Performed by tea masters, the ceremony is a haven of harmony, respect, peace, and purity, and years of training are necessary before one can become a "master." The first school for the tea ceremony was created by Murata Shuko at the end of the fifteenth century, while Kyoto was still the imperial capital. The best-known tea master in Japanese history, however, was without question Sen No Rikyu (1522–91). It was he who imposed the exacting codes of the ceremony and made it into a genuine spiritual rite.

Before beginning the *cha no yu*, participants must give up all negative thoughts. The mind must be filled with humility and serenity. The simplicity and plainness of the décor in the *chashitsu* (tea house)—a *kakemono* (vertical scroll painting) showing a landscape, the *ikebana* (traditional floral arrangement) or a bunch of flowers that varies with the season—paves the path to "the way of tea." Samurai would take off their weapons before entering the house.

The essential articles for any Japanese tea ceremony are:
- the *natsume*: a lacquer caddy containing the *matcha* (tea powder)

The master of the tea
ceremony beats the
matcha with the tea
whip (chasen) to make a
"jade froth."

Facing page:
Chashaku, the bamboo
tea scoop.

- the *chasen*: a bamboo whip for beating the tea. Certain tea masters use each one only once. This *chasen* is made in accordance with precise criteria provided by the tea master who orders it.
- the *chawan*: tea bowl
- the *kama*: a vessel for the hot water
- the *chashaku*: a bamboo scoop used to serve out the correct quantity of tea
- the *hishaku*: a bamboo ladle for taking hot water from the cauldron

The ceremony proceeds as follows. One takes up some hot water with the *hishaku* from the *kama* and pours it into the *chawan*, in which one has already placed the *matcha* using the bamboo *chashaku*. The master then beats the *matcha* with the *chasen*, driving it into a "jade foam." A bowl of tea is then offered to the "first" or "head" guest who tastes it respectfully in little mouthfuls, being careful to suck up the dregs; only then will the master begin preparing for the next guest. The palate is primed to appreciate the bitterness of the tea by consuming sweetmeats containing red beans. This tradition is still very much alive, and the ceremony can be enjoyed in Kyoto, Tokyo, and many other parts of Japan. Three schools specializing in the "way of tea" continue to teach the art of tea making.

Today, Japan is a major producer of green tea with an annual output of eighty thousand tons, making it the sixth largest tea producer in the world. The earliest Japanese plantations, seeded from *Camellia sinensis* brought back from China by Buddhist monks, date from the tenth century.

These plantations still flower in the beautiful province of Uji, located south of Kyoto, as well as in the vast region of Shizuoka, nearer Tokyo, and are marvelously well-tended. The Nagoya region has gained a reputation for its pretty earthenware and stoneware bowls and teapots, and Japan was the first country to manufacture good cast-iron teapots.

In this nation split between modernity and tradition, every conceivable aspect of the art of tea has been elevated to supreme refinement.

Facing page:
Various Japanese teas.

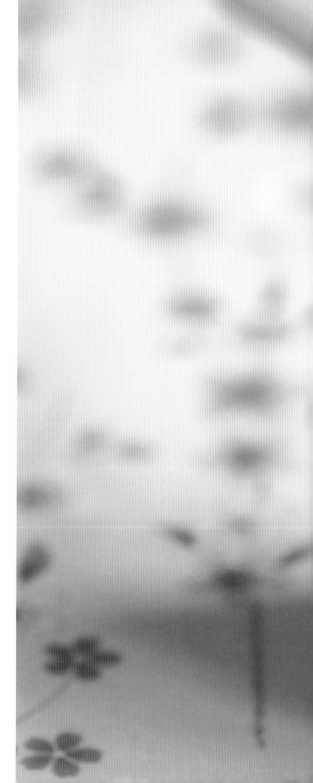

This extract from *The Life of Tea and Spirit of Tea*, by Soshitsu Sen[1] is an evocation of the ever-present quest for simplicity and purity in Japan.

HARMONY, RESPECT, PURITY, AND PEACE

To he who yearns for
The flowers of spring,
Show the young growths
Peeping out from the snow-clad hills…
Tea is nothing other than this:
Heat the water,
Prepare the tea,
And drink it in due form.

This poem says all one needs to know about the tea ceremony.

Facing page:
Matcha tea and chashaku
(scoop for serving tea).

[1] Soshitsu Sen is the fifteenth descendent of a line of great masters of the tea ceremony in Japan: the Urasenke school.

Various Japanese pâtisseries based on red beans. They are eaten with tea to counter their bitterness.

TIBET

Tea (*boeja*) was first imported into Tibet in the seventh century, during the reign of Songtsen Gampo.

Tea at that time was made in China in the form of "pressed" wafers or tablets. Because it was preserved in this manner, it could be readily transported aboard yak caravans and brought back to the towering peaks of Tibet. The nine-hundred-and-fifty-mile (1500-km) journey from the Chinese provinces of Yunnan or Sichuan to Lhassa, at an altitude of well more than sixteen thousand feet (5,000 m), lasted several months.

As soon as tea was introduced in Tibet, the inhabitants began preparing it in a unique fashion. First, the tea has to be "broken," then crushed. It is then boiled in water, with the addition of salt and butter. It can be drunk with milk or eaten with barley flour. Prepared according to this method, this energy-giving beverage is still served to visitors exhausted by the interminable climb.

Facing page:
In Tibet, the pounded tea is boiled and taken with butter and salt.

INDIA

The history of tea in India is closely connected to the history of England. Its culture and development in this country date only from the nineteenth century, yet present-day India is the largest producer of tea in the world, with an output of some nine hundred thousand tons a year. English merchants such as the East India Company—that ensured the trade in tea between China and the West—quickly saw the interest of possessing their own plantations.

By the end of the eighteenth century, tests on growing the *sinensis* tea plant were already being carried out in botanical gardens near Calcutta with encouraging results. It was at the beginning of the nineteenth century, with the clearing of the province of Assam by the Bruce Brothers, however, that another variety of tea plant, *Camellia assamica*, was discovered. *Camellia assamica* grows marvelously well on plains, and its yield is higher than

Facing page:
In Kashmir, tea is drunk with cardamom seeds and crushed almonds.

that of *Camellia sinensis*. The taste of the tea it produces has far more vigor and power.

The first tea council was created in 1834 by Lord Bentick. Tea growing could now start in earnest, with Chinese workmen being persuaded to travel to India to teach its cultivation. In 1839, the Assam Company was set up to be responsible for developing the cultivation of plains tea throughout the entire region. By 1860, there were approximately one hundred and sixty plantations.

The history of the arrival of tea at Darjeeling, an upland region in the far north of India, is quite another story. The Scottish botanist Robert Fortune, born on September 16, 1812, was commissioned by the Royal Horticultural Society to undertake, starting in July 1843, a first voyage to China. Disguised as a Mandarin and with the assistance of a Chinese guide, he journeyed across China for several months and, in spite of threats to life and limb, collected or purchased *sinensis* tea plants from various regions. Early dispatches of these *Camellia sinensis* to Calcutta were a failure, nonetheless, as the delicate young seedlings perished on the long voyage.

In 1848, however, during a second trip, this time on behalf of the British East India Company, Fortune succeeded in "purloining" from China 12,837 nursery tea plants.

The first plantations of *Camellia sinensis* saw the light of day in Darjeeling, in all probability at Puttabong and Tukvar, two prestigious estates that to this day grow teas of excellent quality. By 1850— that is to say scarcely two years later, Darjeeling

contained some eighty tea gardens. The tea produced by this area is considered by many to be the best in the world, and is dubbed by some "the champagne of teas."

India, which regained independence in 1947, today exports the near totality of its production. In India itself, only the worst quality tea is drunk. It is tart-tasting, its leaves are broken, and it is the custom to consume it with milk and spices. In Kashmir, it is taken with cardamom seeds and crushed almonds. In the Punjab in the north of India, it is boiled with milk, and served with pepper or chili.

Nowadays, *chai* (tea) is drunk everywhere in India. It is often served in a simple clay cup which may be smashed after use, thereby ensuring that no member of a lower caste will be able to drink from the same bowl.

Facing page:
Darjeeling F.T.G.F.O.P.

Sri Lanka

Nothing seemed to indicate that Sri Lanka was destined to become the third largest tea-producing country in the world. From the mid-seventeenth to the end of the eighteenth century, the island was occupied by the Dutch, and nobody thought of cultivating the famous *Camellia sinensis* on it. Only once the English had taken over was then-Ceylon transformed first into an island of coffee. Coffee bean production reached levels competitive with Brazil, until the appearance of a terrible fungus that devastated all the island's coffee plantations. Luckily, a few growers had already diversified their crop.

It is to James Taylor (a young Scot who abandoned his family and fatherland to go to Ceylon) that we owe the first tea estate. This young botanist began planting tea from India and China in 1860. In 1872, he invented a machine to roll tea leaves. He never owned an actual plantation, working instead on behalf of the property of Loodecondera for his entire life. When the property was sold off to a bank, James Taylor was dismissed. He passed away in May 1892, aged fifty-seven, probably from disappointment. Certainly, he died without the satisfaction of learning that Ceylon tea would be one of principal "attractions" of the World's Fair at Chicago the following year.

The name of another tea lover and adventurer is forever bound with that of Ceylon tea: Thomas Lipton. In 1890, he bought some plantations there, making his own tea which he exported directly to English consumers, who were already hugely fond of this beverage. He even invented one of its first advertising slogans: "From the tea gardens to the teapot." The first tea board was set up in what was then Ceylon in 1886. At the same time, many "promotional campaigns" for Ceylon tea were organized in Europe.

Since gaining its independence in 1948, Sri Lanka has continued to produce quality tea in every area of the island. Today, the Sri Lanka tea council is extremely dynamic and is present at every European forum in its efforts to show the diversity of its produce. Sri Lanka, which historically has only produced fermented black tea, has begun supplying green and blue-green teas as well. This output, though small at present, will surely increase in future years.

TEA IN WESTERN EUROPE

Tea's long voyage from Asia to the West undoubtedly began in the ninth century. The presence of tea was noted by several Arab travelers in their writings, as it followed the "caravan" route from Canton westward. Marco Polo mentioned it in the thirteenth century, describing it as a drink for women and old men only. In the sixteenth century, intrepid explorers started plying the seas, and the Earth was definitively declared "round." It was by sea, of course, that Portuguese navigators also brought the first cases of tea back to their homeland, which at that time held the important trading post of Macao.

As for the Dutch, in 1602 they founded the first East India Company and by 1606 were importing crates of tea into Europe. Indeed, until about 1660, they exerted a monopoly over Oriental trade. They began by exchanging cases of sage and borage for chests of tea in China and Japan.

In the first part of the seventeenth century, the English preferred to drink coffee. But, after 1660, the English broke off commercial ties with Holland and set up a concern of their own, the British East India Company. By then, tea had made its official entrance in London and at the royal court. Indeed, by 1658, a famous innkeeper by the name of Thomas Garraway was proposing tea in his establishment. At that time, however, tea was mostly regarded as a beverage capable of relieving headaches and treating intestinal problems.

Then, in 1662, the Portuguese princess Catherine of Braganza married Charles II of England and introduced the English court to the concept of teatime. As a dowry, the Infante also brought with her the splendid trading-post of Bombay.

An English poet, Edmund Waller, dedicated the following verses to the queen and the drink she favored:

The best of Queens, the best of herbs, we owe
To that bold nation which the way did show
To the fair region where the sun doth rise [...].

Naturally, the interest and taste Queen Catherine showed for tea spurred English merchants into action, and soon a tea trade was up and running. King Charles II, moreover, reaped considerable income from taxing it. During the eighteenth century, the English unseated the Dutch, gaining a monopoly over trade with China that they preserved until 1834, when the Chinese decided to proscribe all trade with the English. The First Opium War flared up subsequently, in 1839, resulting in the capitulation of China in 1842 and the already mentioned Treaty of Nanking, which opened up five major Chinese trading posts to the English (and handed them the island of Hong Kong).

By then, tea had long become extremely popular in England, overtaking coffee. In 1769, the English already imported nearly two thousand tons of tea. This fragile import, however, was often marred by the long sea voyage from the Orient in damp holds, and traders incurred huge losses. As the nineteenth century progressed it became clear that far faster ships had to be built; the result was construction of the famous sailing ships called clippers, such as the

Facing page: An infusion of Nymphéas, made from a Chinese black tea, flavored with vanilla, rhubarb, and red fruits, with a scattering of helianthus and cornflower petals.

Cutty Sark, a splendid and especially fast clipper that has left its illustrious name in the annals of history.

True races began between the various maritime companies, with bonuses awarded to the winners by merchants in London. In December 1850, however, it was an American clipper, *The Oriental*, which proved the fastest, managing to sail from Hong Kong to London in just ninety-five days. This was a supreme humiliation for the English whose fastest clipper arrived a full fortnight later. These races steadily increased in competitiveness until 1866, when a particularly famous event took place. Several clippers, leaving from the far-away port of Fuzhou in Fujian, arrived in London with only minutes separating them.

In 1869, however, the opening of the Suez Canal brought a sudden halt to this little "game," and over time clippers were replaced by steamers in the transport of tea.

Facing page:
The blend of sweet
vanilla, tart rhubarb,
and soft red fruit makes
for a marvelous
combination.

THE HISTORY OF THE GREAT ENGLISH BRANDS

Lipton

Thomas Lipton was born in Glasgow, Scotland, in 1850. He was the son of Irish emigrants who fled their native land in 1848 at the time of the Great Famine. If his world in Scotland was limited to the port and its brick-built tenements stained black with soot, Lipton had his eyes firmly on sailing the seven seas. He embarked for America, returning home a few years later with some money saved up for his beloved parents. In 1871, he opened a small grocery store in which he applied the innovative commercial techniques he had witnessed in America. Soon, Glasgow was filled with talk of Lipton's store. Through bypassing middlemen, he could stock his shop at the lowest rates, and customers flooded in, attracted by the advantageous prices he was thereby able to offer. He was also the first to use "sandwich-men" for advertising and to paint his trucks to reflect his brand.

By 1891, Lipton possessed no less than two-hundred outlets. Around this time, he decided to buy land in what was then Ceylon, hoping to cultivate *Camellia sinensis* after the coffee plantations there had been devastated by the ravages of fungal disease. He, thus, became a tea producer, importer, and retailer all rolled into one, overseeing the entire trade from "tea garden to teapot." Tea was becoming democratized, and by 1895 Thomas Lipton was official purveyor to Queen Victoria. He was even knighted three years later. He was also the first to

Facing page:
Sir Thomas Lipton.

pack and sell tea in tea boxes on which he provided instructions for correct brewing.

Thomas Lipton's other passion remained sailing. He never won any of the five America's Cups he entered but, in his eyes, the main thing was to take part and, by so doing, publicize his name was widely as possible. He died in 1931, immensely wealthy and famous throughout the world.

Twinings

Thomas Twinings opened a first coffeehouse in 1706 called *Tom's*, near the docks just outside the City (the old city of London, now London's financial district). In 1717, he opened a new shop, *The Golden Lyon*, this time especially for selling coffee and tea. Then, at the very beginning of the eighteenth century, he set up the very first store devoted to the sale of tea alone. It was Twinings that invented selling tea by the cup and who packaged the first tea bags, weighing around three and a half ounces (100 g), for retail. His motto was "Tea and Sympathy." Twinings is still a well-known brand, recognized worldwide.

Fortnum and Mason

This brand was born from the meeting in London in 1705 of William Fortnum and Hugh Mason. Together, they created a luxury delicatessen whose ambition was to supply anything and everything to the rich aristocracy. By fulfilling the dreams of those at court, they made a fortune. Of course, tea—then extremely popular at the royal court—played a significant part in their business.

Fortnum and Mason still exists today. Many are those who have appreciated its famous cucumber sandwiches and luxurious green-painted tearoom.

Earl Grey

The Prime Minister of Britain from 1830 to 1834, Charles Grey, the Second Earl Grey, was a keen tea lover. According to legend, one day, while he was sipping his favorite beverage, he was given a bergamot. He ended up cutting off a piece and dropping it in his tea. It was delicious. Thus was born one of the most famous teas in the world: Earl Grey.

THE ART OF TEA IN ENGLAND

One cannot dissociate the history of tea in England from how it is enjoyed there: teatime has become enshrined in ritual in England, complete with the tea-cozy to keep the tea inside the pot piping hot and, of course, the teapot. Not forgetting scones, buns, pancakes, and muffins: delicious eaten with Seville orange marmalade and invented especially to accompany tea. English teapots also reached heights of elaborateness. Sheffield manufacturers were famous for silver plate, while Wedgwood and Leeds made the English into the creators of the most beautiful teapots in Europe. The English were also the first to go in for eccentric shapes for teapots, very popular in the 1930s and given a new lease on life at the beginning of the 1980s. Makers like Tony Wood, Arthur Wood, and Price of Kensington certainly did not lack imagination: teapots in the shape of a cottage, a hen, a pig,

FORTNUM & MASON™
ESTABLISHED 1707

Green - Teas

GREEN EARL GREY

A CLASSIC BLEND OF GREEN TEA
WITH OIL OF BERGAMOT

NET WEIGHT
POIDS NET 125 g 4.4 oz

a cat, and even of a convertible car were brought out. If not invariably practical, these teapots have collectors falling over each other for them today.

Many people in England continue to drink tea throughout the day, starting with breakfast, where they tend to enjoy it rather strong, very dark, with a dash of cooling milk. They like to drink tea both at work and at home, with family or friends, and remain the second greatest consumers of tea in Europe (just behind Ireland), with more than six pounds (2.8 kg) a year bought per person.

Here is an extract from Henri de Parville's *Annales politiques et littéraires* dated January 5, 1896:

An English newspaper informs us that the English are no longer content with merely drinking tea with their 'five o'clock': they have started smoking it. It appears that it has become fashionable lunacy to light up green tea in the form of cigarettes. A considerable proportion of the followers of this singular pastime are women of condition and intellectual distinction. The steam emerging from the teapot now competes with blue cigarette smoke and drawing-rooms are filled with a scented mist…. By all accounts, it improves conversation and makes talking ill of one's neighbor even more delightful.

FRANCE

Tea made its appearance in France at the very beginning of the seventeenth century. It is said that Mazarin treated the aches and pains of his dropsy with it. The beverage was by and large the preserve of the court. Regular drinkers ranged from the scurrilous poet Paul Scarron to the distinguished bluestocking Madame de Sévigné. On August 27, 1664, at the behest of Louis XIV, the Sun King, First Minister Colbert founded the Compagnie Française des Indes Orientales (the French Company of the East Indies), whose goal was "to sail and negotiate from the Cape of Good Hope to well-nigh all the Indies and over every Oriental sea." It was deemed paramount to fight and compete with the Dutch and English maritime companies, and a monopoly over trade in France was granted to it for no less than fifty years. For more than a century, the company's headquarters were located at L'Orient in the south of Brittany, in the French regional department of Morbihan. The town of Lorient (as it is now spelt) still possesses its famous "quays of the Indies" from which the company's vessels weighed anchor and, after a long and perilous voyage, the ships unloaded their cargo of tea, spices, porcelain, silk and cotton fabrics at these very same docks.

When the French Company of the East Indies was founded, it was agreed that sailors would embark for a minimum of one year's service. The green tea these sailors brought back was at the time primarily considered in France as a medicinal drink, which apothecaries sold at a high price. At the court of France, it was taken frequently by noble ladies such as Madame de la Martinière, to whom we probably owe the "discovery" of tea with milk: concerned for the fate of her priceless porcelain, she hit upon the idea of pouring cold milk at the bottom of the cup to cool the boiling tea.

The royal porcelain manufactories at Sèvres and Vincennes deployed great ingenuity in creating

splendid tea services, including teapots, cups, and sugar bowls.

In the course of the eighteenth century, French interest in tea increased steadily. Abbé Raynal explained the vogue for Chinese tea thus: "The fashion for this infusion did not spring from some whimsical folly. Water is brackish, unpalatable, and unhealthy throughout the empire, especially in low-lying provinces." Of all the means imagined to combat this water problem, the use of tea was the only one to prove completely successful.

Ceylon tearooms were one of the hits at the Universal Exhibition of 1900 in Paris, and their exoticism and refinement proved a magnet to elegant society. The French writer Jean Lorrain described the phenomenon as follows:

For tea, there is, behind the Ceylon pavilion, a refreshing, calm little place in the Trocadéro, where tea is taken in the shade at small tables set around a kiosk. The lacquered pillars and colored mats ringed by a palisade, all so neatly arranged, are a delight to the eye. Wearing white piqué jackets buttoned over their aprons to form a skirt, the slender yet strapping fellows, with bronze faces and long black hair twisted into a bun are somewhat disconcerting with their shining enamel-like eyes; they are assisted in their service by barmaids, fresh and pink. The spot is already well-frequented and has been adopted by elegant and inquisitive women hypnotized by the elastic stride and the velvety pupils of the men of Ceylon. One of them was pointed out to me whose conquests are beyond counting.

By the mid-nineteenth century there were, however, already a few rare tea outlets in Paris. In 1854, Mariage Frères opened a store devoted to tea in Paris's Marais district. Now world-famous, this firm still today perhaps represents more than any other the art of tea drinking in France.

During the twentieth century, Paris witnessed the arrival of two more fine tea firms: Betjeman and Barton, who founded, on their arrival in France in 1919, The English Tea House near the Madeleine Church in Paris, a splendid place that showed Parisians how to take tea English-style, and the celebrated Russian tea house of Kousmichoff, which established itself in Paris's seventeenth *arrondissement* in 1920. Founded in St. Petersburg in 1867, the Kousmichoff tea concern first appeared in London in 1917, before ending up in Paris in 1920. Since its creation by Pavel Michailovitch Kousmichoff, the firm has won many awards for the quality and originality of its teas. In 1911, it was singled out at the London International Exhibition, and it carried off a gold medal in 1927 in Hamburg. That same year, Kousmichoff was awarded the gold medal at the Exhibition of Cuisine and Gastronomy in Paris. It has been singularly successful in bringing Russian tea-drinking customs to France.

Since 1980, other French brands have been created. The Contes de Thé was founded in 1986 in the Saint-Germain district of Paris, and for ten years now has been exporting to Japan, as well as to such countries as Italy, Belgium, Switzerland, Portugal.

And, so, the art of taking tea *à la française* is now also being exported worldwide. Today, every French city has its own tea retailer. From north to south and from east to west, one can buy loose tea of excellent quality. And the French are consuming more and more tea: almost ten ounces (275 g) per year per capita, to be exact. They are particularly fond of scented green teas. Tearooms too are springing up all over the place, serving quality brews of great tea.

The creativity shown by certain French *pâtissiers*, who use tea in the preparation of new pastries, is also to be applauded: almond *financiers* made with *matcha*, fruit cakes with Earl Grey, and "Russian-flavor" *madeleines*, to name but a few.

TEA IN EASTERN EUROPE

RUSSIA

Tea made its entrance into Russia at the court of Tsar Mikhail Feodorovich in 1638. In exchange for some sable fur, Khan Altyn of Mongolia had sent the tsar a case containing one hundred and fifty pounds (65 kilos) of tea. The court was at first perplexed and put out—could this be an affront to the tsar? Having learned of this potentially dangerous diplomatic incident, the khan hurriedly dispatched a tea specialist to Moscow. He taught the court how to prepare what was soon acknowledged as a marvelous drink. The tsar himself found it easy to digest and flavorsome, and so the taste for tea spread through the Russian upper crust like wildfire. Of course, given its scarcity and consequent high commercial value, it was initially reserved for the court and the higher echelons of the aristocracy, just as it was in Europe. The nobility often drank it for medicinal purposes, and it was credited with curing many maladies.

Gradually, towards the end of the seventeenth century, a Russian tea trade was organized. The number of tea fanciers was growing, and Moscow merchants went more and more regularly to Peking to get their hands on the precious leaves their clients desired. In spite of the danger and difficulty of what was a perilous voyage, dealing in tea proved just too lucrative to ignore. In the eighteenth century, a "tea route" carved its way from Peking to Moscow through the Gobi Desert, across passes, marshes, and steppes, as well as via Siberia, to Lake Baikal and banks of the Volga. Caravans numbering about thirty camels conveyed the precious cargo back to Russia, packed in bundles attached to the sides of the wooden saddles. Little by little, the means of transport improved. The word "caravan," though, was still used, even if the tea traveled in carts drawn by oxen or horses. This method of transport possessed the disadvantage of being slow, expensive, and unsafe, but it remained the best, as tea transported by land kept far better. The tea conveyed in ships to Western Europe in damp holds, during a voyage that lasted for months, could not hope to be of the same quality. Sometimes, it even rotted.

At the Russian court, tea drinking became ever more ritualized. The tsar and his family drank it every afternoon around five, often with pastries and other delicacies. Many retailers and tearooms opened up, first in Moscow and, then, in St. Petersburg, when Tsar Peter I settled his court there.

At that time, Russians also drank a hot or cold beverage, composed of water with honey and various spices according to the region, called *sbiten*. To keep this drink hot during winter, salesmen used kettles fitted with a pipe that they placed over burning embers. Manufactured in the Urals, it was this *sbitennik*, as such kettles were called, which was to be the precursor of the samovar. Tsar Peter I granted the privilege of working the iron ore at Suksun to the manufactory of Demidov, and the first samovar was made there in 1730. But, thereafter, thanks to its proximity to Moscow, the region of Tula became the center of samovar manufacture. The demand was such that, in 1850, there were already more than twenty-eight samovar factories

Facing page:
In Moscow, they enjoy their tea strong and vigorous. To reduce its bitterness, they have developed the practice of adding jam, lemon, or even cream.

in Russia, with an output of some one hundred and twenty thousand units a year. The "kings" of the samovar were at that time the Brothers Batashev, suppliers to the court of the tsar and to the king of Spain. Of limitless imagination and creativity, their samovars were veritable works of art and vastly expensive. Often decorated with gold or silver, they were made in the shape of Empire vases, balls, firkins, and even pears.

The typical Russian manner of drinking tea was entirely original and unique. First, a highly concentrated tea—a kind of tea extract—was prepared in a small pot. This teapot was then placed on top of the samovar to keep it hot. One then served oneself a little tea liquor in a glass, adding hot water from the samovar. The favorite of the Asian part of Russia was (unfermented) green tea, while black tea was preferred in the European zone. In Moscow, it was taken extremely strong and bitter, its tang mitigated by the addition of jam, lemon, or even cream. Sugar was not put in the cup but placed in the mouth, and the tea was drunk through it.

Nevertheless, it was not before the nineteenth century that *sbiten* was generally replaced by tea in all parts of Russia. The court of the tsar then lived in St. Petersburg, which was filled with tea stores. Pavel Michailovitch Kousmichoff, already mentioned in relation to France, founded his first shop there in 1867. He very quickly became official tea supplier to the court, gaining an exellent reputation for the quality of his teas and the creativity of his blends. He was the inventor in 1880 of the tsar's adored "Bouquet de Fleurs," also known as no. 108, a black

tea with bergamot, citrus fruits, and flowers. He was also already composing "classic" or original blends of tea to be taken at different times of day. The no. 24, or "morning tea," was a clever mix of black teas from China, Ceylon, and India; the no. 50, or "evening tea," was composed of black teas from India and China with a lower theine content.

Kousmichoff then went on to create a tea with a "Russian taste" called "Prince Vladimir." This black tea is delicately scented with citrus, vanilla, and spices. Other blends followed, like Anastasia and Troika. During the reign of Tsar Nicolas II, the Kousmichoff house possessed about fifteen outlets in Russia, and its reputation was unassailable. Fleeing the Revolution of 1917, Kousmichoff eventually settled in Paris, where his firm remains a benchmark in the world of tea. So-called "Russian taste" teas continue to hold their own. Even the enchanting names under which they are marketed are an invitation to dream and travel: Douchka, Anouchka, Baïkal, Saint Petersbourg, Tsar Alexander, Tea on the Volga.

One more little anecdote: from the beginning of the nineteenth century, a golden age for tea when the drink was becoming widely available throughout Russia, the word for a "tip" was none other than *na chai*: "for the tea."

Facing page:
Tea boxes, Russia.

AFGHANISTAN

Afghanistan was a stopover on the Silk Road. Tea was served in the open air, attracting pilgrims and caravaneers who would meet under vast tents for a cup or two. These "tea houses" were called *chaikhana* (rest houses) and were a hive of activity. Musicians and singers flocked to them, and they were also places where merchants could discuss business and nomads could squat chatting quietly, glad of a pause on their interminable travels. Tea was served in blue or red teapots imported from Russia. As time went on, a number of cottage industries manufacturing these teapots sprang up locally.

Tea is still held in the utmost respect and is served by nomads as a mark of hospitality. To refuse a cup would be considered sacrilege.

MOROCCO

From 1854 to 1856, the Crimean War saw France, England, and Russia at loggerheads. English ships were blockaded in the strategic Straits of Gibraltar just south of Spain and near the Moroccan coast. The English offered the sultan and his entourage valuable cargo, including chests of tea.

The Moroccans, who had the habit of drinking infusions of mint leaves all day, added a pinch of green tea to their favorite beverage and pronounced it delicious. The Moroccan affair with tea had begun. Following this "love at first taste," in 1856 Morocco signed its earliest commercial treaty with the European powers. Today, the Moroccans are one of the greatest consumers of green Gunpowder tea in the world: six and a half pounds (3 kg) a year per person.

Everywhere in Morocco today, in the countryside as well as in large cities, you will be greeted with a cup or glass of tea as a sign of welcome. A tradition embraced by all, the tea ceremony takes place in every echelon of society.

If you ever have the honor of taking tea with a middle-class family in Morocco, you will notice:
- a first tray on which will be placed tea-glasses, one or two silver-plated teapots, and a large metal container;
- a second silver-plated tray with a sugar bowl, a sugarloaf, a little copper hammer, and a dish full of fresh mint, as well as a small tea box containing the famous Gunpowder, a green tea rolled into a shape like buckshot. In winter, when fresh mint is unavailable, they use *shiba* or fresh wormwood.

The two trays are covered with two gossamer-like muslin napkins, often prettily embroidered. The lady of the house presents you with a little flask of water and orange flower to freshen up your hands or, if you wish, to flavor the tea. Now the ceremony proper can start.

First of all, one pours boiling water into the teapot and rinses it round; only then does one put the tea in, together with a generous helping of fresh mint from which as many of the bitter stems as possible have been removed. (Before the appearance of the kettle, the water was heated in a cauldron over burning embers.) Then one pours onto this preparation the equivalent of a glass of water. The mixture is shaken, and the infusion thrown into a large glass. Using the little copper hammer, one breaks off a little sugar and puts it in the teapot.

Facing page:
Tea only appeared in Morocco at the end of the nineteenth century. Today, Moroccans consume about six and a half pounds (3 kg) of tea per person a year.

Scalding water is then poured on to the tea and allowed to stand for around four minutes. When it comes to serving the tea in the small glasses, care is taken to lift the teapot up so as to oxygenate the boiled water, and so make the tea more digestible.

In the countryside, tea is prepared more simply: the water, tea, the sprig of mint, and the sugar are put in an enamel teapot and placed directly on the fire. The brew obtained is far stronger. The more south one travels in Morocco, the stronger the tea gets. An offer of tea in Morocco is considered a heartfelt gift.

Facing page:
In Morocco, tea may
be taken with a few
pine nuts.

TEA IN THE UNITED STATES

The earliest European colonists made landfall on the eastern seaboard. Britain was careful to ensure it had a monopoly over trade and supplies. In spite of protests from the colonists, England's monarch, whose treasuries were often empty, regularly ordered increases in taxes and excise, including on tea. The resulting sense of injustice culminated in the first revolt against English tyranny. On December 16, 1773, in Boston, Massachusetts, insurrectionists hurled more than three hundred chests of tea into the sea, the cargo from three heavy ships anchored in the port. This episode, now immortalized as the Boston Tea Party, marked the first step on the march to independence for the American colonies.

During the nineteenth century Americans built clippers to transport tea and spices to their young country. Today, Americans consume around twenty-one ounces (600 g) of tea a year per person.

Americans were probably the first to make ice tea, a drink that is still incredibly popular to this day. To make a good ice tea, put three or four ounces (about 10 g) of the tea of your choice, either green or traditional "black," in a jug. Pour in a liter of cold water and allow it steep in the refrigerator all night. Then, strain it and serve in pretty glasses. It can even be adorned with fruit peel. Americans also enjoy flavored teas, and both teas and other plants with reported health-giving properties. The Rooibos, or red tea, of South Africa has met with notable success.

CONCLUSION

After five thousand years of history, tea is today the second most frequently consumed beverage in the world after water. Almost all the secrets of growing and making it, which until the nineteenth century were the monopoly of China, are widely known. Laboratories around the globe undertake research on its health benefits.

As well as a voyage of discovery, tea is and will remain an opportunity for sharing. Nothing is more extraordinary than to watch tea leaves unfurl as the water soaks into them, to see the color of the brew change, to bring one's lips to the cup, and to close one's eyes and savor the taste.

BUYER'S GUIDE

CANADA

Épicerie Européenne
560, rue Saint-Jean
Quebec
QC G1R 1P6
Tel.: +1 (418) 529-4847
Fax: +1 (418) 529-0368
www.epicerie-
europeenne.com

Fouvrac
1451, avenue Laurier est
Montreal
QC H2J 1H8
Tel.: +1 (514) 522-9993

Nectar Fine Teas
1250 Wellington Street West
Ottawa, ON K1Y 3A4
Tel.: +1 (613) 759-8327

FRANCE

Kusmi Tea
75, avenue Niel
75017 Paris
Tel.: +33 (0)1 42 27 91 46
www.kusmitea.com

Hôtel Lutetia (tea room)
45, boulevard Raspail
75006 Paris
Tel.: +33 (0) 1 49 54 46 46
Fax: +33 (0)1 49 54 46 00
www.lutetia-paris.com

La Grande Epicerie de Paris
38, rue de Sèvres
75007 Paris
Tel.: +33 (0) 1 44 39 81 00

Fax : +33 (0) 1 44 39 81 17
www.lagrandeepicerie.fr

Les Contes de Thé
60, rue du Cherche-Midi
75006 Paris
Tel.: +33 (0)1 45 49 45 96

JAPAN

Iwai Bussan
335 Higashi
Kamiyanagi-Cho
Karasumadori
Kyoto

UNITED KINGDOM

Claris's (tea room)
1-3 High Street
Biddenden
Kent, TN27 8AL
Tel.: +44 (0) 15 80 291 025
Fax: +44 (0) 15 80 291 025
www.collectablegifts.net

The Dorchester Hotel
(tea room)
Park Lane
London W1A 2HJ
Tel.: + 44 (0) 20 76 298 888
Fax: +44 (0) 20 74 090 114
www.thedorchester.com

Fortnum & Mason
181 Piccadilly
London W1A 1ER
Tel.: +44 (0) 20 77 348 040
Fax: +44 (0) 20 74 373 278
www.fortnumandmason.com

Grey's Teas
33 Green Lane
Warwick CV34 5BP
Tel.: +44 (0) 19 26 419 180
www.greysteas.co.uk

Harrods Ltd
87-135 Brompton Road
Knightsbridge
London SW1X 7XL
Tel.: +44 (0) 20 77 301 234
Fax: +44 (0) 20 72 256 633
www.harrods.com

Haskett's Tea & Coffee Shop
(tea room)
86b South Street
Dorking
Surrey, RH4 2EW
Tel.: +44 (0) 13 06 885 833

The London Tea Company
Central House
1 Ballards Lane
Finchley
London N3 1LQ
Tel.: +44 (0) 20 83 498 089
www.londontea.co.uk

Mighty Leaf Teas
Somerset Distribution UK Ltd.
4 Damson Garth
Lund
Driffield YO25 9TH
Tel.: +44 (0) 13 77 217 793
www.mightyleafteas.co.uk

**Mount Fuji International
Limited**
Felton Butler
Shrewsbury SY4 1AS
Tel.: +44 (0) 17 43 741 169

Fax.: +44 (0) 17 43 741 650
www.mountfuji.co.uk

Northern Tea Merchants
193 Chatsworth Road
Brampton
Chesterfield, S40 2BA
Tel.: +44 (0) 12 46 232 600
Fax: +44 (0) 12 46 555 991
www.northern-tea.com

Nothing But Tea
Unit 1, Grisedale Court
Woburn Road Industrial
Estate
Kempston
Bedford MK42 7EE
Tel.: +44 (0) 12 34 853 855
Fax: +44 (0) 12 34 853 232
www.nbtea.co.uk

Robert Wilson Ceylon Teas
Stonehaven
Nuttree
North Perrott
Crewkerne
Somerset TA18 7SX
Tel.: +44 (0) 14 60 775 08
www.wilstea.com

The Tea Shop
6 Polmorla Road
Wadebridge
Cornwall, PL27 7ND
Tel.: +44 (0) 12 08 813 331

UNITED STATES

The Fairmont Hotel
950 Mason Street
San Francisco, CA 94108

Tel.: +1 (415) 772-5000
Fax: +1 (415) 772-5013
www.fairmont.com/sanfrancisco

Harney & Sons (tea shop and tasting room)
Main Street
The Railroad Plaza
Millerton, NY 12546
Tel.: +1 (518) 789-2121
Fax: +1 (518) 789-2100
www.harney.com

Ito En
822 Madison Avenue
New York, NY 10021
Tel.: +1 (212) 988-7111
Fax : +1 (212) 570-4500
www.itoen.com

Janam Indian Tea
353 Grove Street
Jersey City, NJ 07302
Tel.: +1 (201) 432-4TEA
Fax: +1 (202) 432-4834
www.janamtea.com

Leaves Pure Tea
7435 East Tierra Buena Lane
Scottsdale, AZ 85260
Tel.: +1 (877) 532-8378
www.leaves.com

Le Palais des Thés
401 North Canyon Drive
Beverly Hills, CA 90210
Tel.: +1 (310) 271-7922
www.palaisdesthes.com

La Société du Thé
2708 Lyndale Avenue South
Minneapolis, MN 55408
Tel.: +1 (612) 871-5148

Fax: +1 (612) 874-0239
www.la-societe-du-the.com

Mark T. Wendell Tea Company
50 Beharrell Street
P.O. Box 1312
West Concord, MA 01742
Tel.: +1 (978) 369-3709
Fax: +1 (978) 369-7972
www.marktwendell.com

Serendipitea
32-29 Greenpoint Avenue
Long Island City, NY 11101
Tel: +1 (888) 832-5433
Fax: +1 (718) 752-0333
www.serendipitea.com

Shan Shui Teas
1847 Monroe Street NW
Washington, DC 20010
Tel.: +1 (202) 258-5280
Fax: +1 (240) 465-2192
www.shanshuiteas.com

Shizuoka Green Tea
20651 Golden Springs Road, Suite 271
Walnut, CA 91789
Tel.: +1 (909) 598-9255
Fax: +1 (909) 598-9255
www.shizuokatea.com

Special Teas
500 Long Beach Blvd.
Stratford, CT 06615
Tel.: +1 (888) 365-6983
Fax: +1 (203) 375-6820
www.specialteas.com

Stash Tea Co.
7250 S.W. Durham Road

Tigard, OR 97224
UNITED STATES
Tel.: +1 (503) 603-9905
www.stashtea.com

Thompson's Fine Teas
152 Old Camp Road
Meridianville, AL 35759
Tel.: +1 (256) 828-6615
www.fineteas.co

True Tea
Mandalay Place
3930 Las Vegas Blvd. S.
Las Vegas, NV 89119
Tel.: +1 (702) 632-9358
www.inpursuitoftea.com

T Salon & T Emporium
11 East 20th Street
New York, NY 10003
Tel.: +1 (212) 358-0506
Fax: +1 (212) 358-0511
www.tsalon.com

The Waldorf Astoria
(tea room)
Cocktail Terrace
301 Park Avenue
New York, NY 10022
Tel.: +1 (212)-872-4818

Yogi Tea
Tel.: +1 (815) 372-4485
www.yogitea.com

AKNOWLEDGMENTS

The author and publishers would like to thank the following for providing material for this book:

Bernardaud
11, rue Royale, 75008 Paris
Tel.: +33 (0) 1 47 42 82 66
www.bernardaud.fr

C.F.O.C.
170, boulevard Haussmann, 75008 Paris
Tel.: +33 (0)1 53 53 40 80
www.compagniefrancaisedelorientetdelachine.com

Mariage Frères
Tel.: +33 (0)1 43 47 18 54
www.mariagefreres.com

Kusmi
75, avenue Niel, 75017 Paris
Tel.: +33 (0)1 42 27 91 46
and 56, rue de Seine
75006 Paris
Tel.: +33 (0)8 92 35 01 45
www.kusmitea.com

Wedgwood chez Old England
12, boulevard des Capucines, 75009 Paris
Tel.: +33 (0)1 47 42 81 99
www.wedgwood.com

Les Contes de Thé
60, rue du Cherche-Midi, 75006 Paris
Tel.: +33 (0) 1 47 42 81 99

Muji
Tel.: +33 (0)1 41 83 70 93
www.mujionline.co.uk

Yodoya
6-8, rue Saint-Gilles, 75003 Paris
Tel.: +33 (0)1 48 87 23 05
www.parisyodoya.com

Minamoto Kitchoan
17, place de la Madeleine, 75008 Paris
Tel.: +33 (0) 1 40 06 91 28
www.kitchoan.com

More information about many of the specialty teas in this book can be obtained from:

Les Contes du Thé
60, rue du Cherche-midi
75006 Paris
France
Tel.: +33 (0)1 45 49 45 96